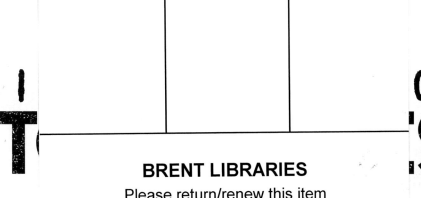

BRENT LIBRARIES

Please return/renew this item
by the last date shown.
Books may also be renewed by
phone or online.
Tel: 0333 370 4700
On-line www.brent.gov.uk/libraryservice

D0657880

raintree 🍃

9112000357063

Raintree is an imprint of Capstone Global Library Limited, a company incorporated in England and Wales having its registered office at 264 Banbury Road, Oxford, OX2 7DY – Registered company number: 6695582

www.raintree.co.uk
myorders@raintree.co.uk

Text © Capstone Global Library Limited 2017
The moral rights of the proprietor have been asserted.

Edited by Alesha Sullivan
Designed by Steve Mead
Picture research by Morgan Walters
Production by Laura Manthe
Printed and bound in India.

ISBN 978 1 4747 3512 4 (hardback)
21 20 19 18 17
10 9 8 7 6 5 4 3 2 1

ISBN 978 1 4747 3516 2 (paperback)
22 21 20 19 18
10 9 8 7 6 5 4 3 2 1

British Library Cataloguing in Publication Data
A full catalogue record for this book is available from the British Library.

Photo Credits
Capstone Press, 6; Capstone Studio: Karon Dubke, 27; Dreamstime: Kathryn Sidenstricker, Cover; Getty Images: AFP, 4, 5, Chris Clor, 13, New York Public Library, 19, Jim Reed, 25; iStockphoto: sshepard, 15; Newscom: Shariful Islam Xinhua News Agency, 20; Shutterstock: Benjamin B, 29, Dean Kerr, 16, Dustie, Cover, Ernest R. Prim, 23, Justin Hobson, 11, Minerva Studio, 8, Nik Merkulov, (grunge texture) design element throughout, cover

CONTENTS

A PATH OF DEVASTATION

It was 26 April 1989. The country of Bangladesh was suffering from a major drought. The president asked the people to pray for rain. Just hours later the worst tornado in the world's history touched down in the Manikganj district. The tornado swept eastwards, creating a path of destruction that was 16 kilometres (10 miles) long and 1.6 kilometres (1 mile) wide. Bangladesh is one of the most heavily populated countries in the world. Most of its people are poor and live in weak shelters. The tornado destroyed every building within 6 square kilometres (2.5 square miles). Twenty villages were destroyed, and 1,300 people died. Heavy rains and hail pummelled the district, and most of the people's crops were destroyed.

People in Bangladesh walk near ruins in April 1989 after a deadly tornado ripped through their city.

Tornadoes are one of the world's deadliest natural disasters. They often strike with very little warning. They can destroy everything in their paths, tossing buildings and cars into the air and flattening houses. For people in many parts of the world, the sound of a tornado warning siren is one of the most frightening sounds they'll ever hear.

TORNADO BASICS

The sky turns dark in the distance. The clouds above echo with low rumbles of thunder. Thunderstorms bring rain, thunder and lightning. Heavy downpours, strong winds and hail are also possible. And a few thunderstorms bring something else – tornadoes. But how does a thunderstorm lead to the formation of a tornado? First, it's important to understand how thunderstorms develop.

THUNDERSTORMS

1

Thunderstorms form when warm, moist air rises. An updraught of wind pushes the warm air high into the sky. The water vapour in the air cools and **condenses**, forming water droplets and a cloud. As more heat rises, a huge **cumulonimbus cloud** forms.

As water droplets in the cloud increase, the cloud can no longer hold in the moisture. The water falls as rain or hail. The air moving with the precipitation is called a downdraught. The downdraught is made of cool air. As the storm grows, more updraughts of wind and downdraughts may form.

2

DOWNDRAUGHT

UPDRAUGHT

3

A thunderstorm usually dies within 30 minutes. By this time the rain and downdraught have usually cooled the air around the storm. Then there is no more warm air feeding the storm with moisture.

condense change from gas to liquid; water vapour condenses into liquid water

cumulonimbus cloud cloud that produces a thunderstorm

Supercells

Not every thunderstorm generates tornadoes. Monstrous storms called supercells are the storms that most often cause tornadoes. These storms have strong winds that can create a swirling column of air. This rotating column of air is called a mesocyclone. The mesocyclone is typically 3.2 to 16 kilometres (2 to 10 miles) wide. It can reach 15,240 metres (50,000 feet) into the sky. In approximately three out of 10 supercells, the mesocyclone forms a tornado.

The elevated winds in a supercell keep the storm going. The high-level wind blows faster than the wind below. This causes the supercell to lean forwards. As the storm leans, the two types of winds are pulled apart. Because the downdraught winds and updraught winds are separated, the updraught winds do not cool down. Warm, moist air keeps feeding the storm, so the storm doesn't die out quickly. A supercell can last for hours.

a supercell

Funnel clouds

If a spinning mesocyclone starts reaching towards the ground, it is called a **funnel cloud**. And if the funnel cloud touches the ground, its name changes to a tornado. When a tornado moves across land, it picks up **debris** with its strong rotating winds. A tornado can travel several kilometres across land. It may have a straight path or a curved path. A tornado's unpredictability makes it very dangerous. It can cause a huge amount of **destruction** in a short amount of time.

Scientists have several ideas about how tornadoes form. One idea is that the mesocyclone moves downwards when the winds beneath it are weak. The slow-moving air below the mesocyclone is drawn upwards and starts to spin. The spinning column then grows larger, pulling the air lower until it touches the ground.

A sinking current of air at the back of the storm may also play a role in the formation of a tornado. This downdraught of dry air moves towards the ground. As it moves, it may wrap around the spinning mesocyclone and pull it down. The rotating column of air stretches and gets thinner. Finally, the mesocyclone reaches the ground.

funnel cloud cone-shaped cloud that is usually a visible part of a tornado; a funnel cloud is wide at the top and narrow at the bottom

debris scattered pieces of something that has been destroyed or broken

destruction what happens when something is badly destroyed

A tornado swept through Elie, Manitoba, in Canada in 2007.

TORNADO ALLEYS

There are places in the world that are more likely to have tornadoes. The United States experiences the biggest, most deadly tornadoes. More than 75 per cent of the world's tornadoes happen in the United States. They are especially likely to happen in "Tornado Alley". This is a name given to the area of the United States that includes the states of Texas, Iowa, Nebraska, Kansas and Ohio. Tornadoes are common in this area because the land is flat. There are no mountains to stop warm, moist air from the Gulf of Mexico from moving north. It meets cooler, dry air coming from Canada. The meeting point of cool air and warm air makes thunderstorms more likely to develop.

FACT

About 100 tornadoes are reported in Canada each year. Most occur in the south-central part of the country. Tornado season in Canada is from April to September.

Other places that see a large number of tornadoes are Russia, Canada and Europe. The United Kingdom is sometimes called "the world's tornado alley". The UK is hit by more than 30 tornadoes each year. On one single day in the UK in 1981, 105 tornadoes were reported. However, most of them were not large enough to cause extensive damage. Tornadoes in the UK usually develop along long, narrow storms that form along cold fronts. Tornadoes along cold fronts are typically weaker than tornadoes formed from supercells, such as in the United States.

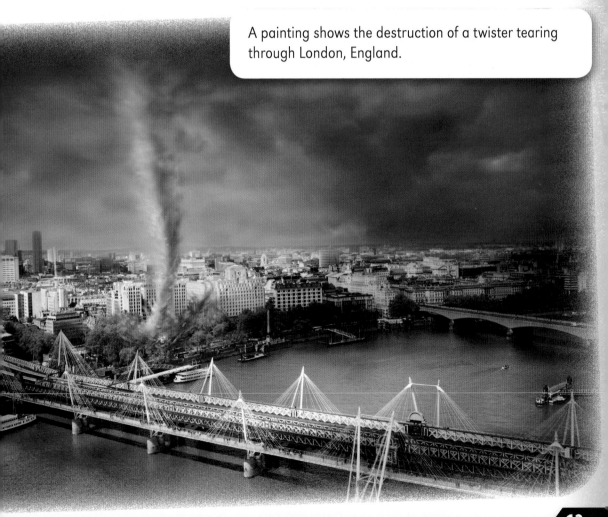

A painting shows the destruction of a twister tearing through London, England.

SIZING UP A TORNADO

Weather experts have a system for classifying the strength of a tornado. Tornadoes are measured by their wind speed. Researchers can estimate a tornado's wind speed by the damage it causes. They consider damage to buildings, power lines, trees and other structures.

Experts in the United States use this information to rank the tornado using the Enhanced Fujita (EF) Scale. The scale measures from 0 to 5. The more destructive the tornado, the higher the number. An EF1 tornado has wind gust estimates of 140 to 180 kilometres (86 to 110 miles) per hour. An EF5 tornado has gusts of more than 320 kilometres (200 miles) per hour. Most tornadoes are an EF1.

EF Rating	wind gust (kph)
5	over 320
4	267-319
3	219-266
2	181-218
1	140-180
0	105-139

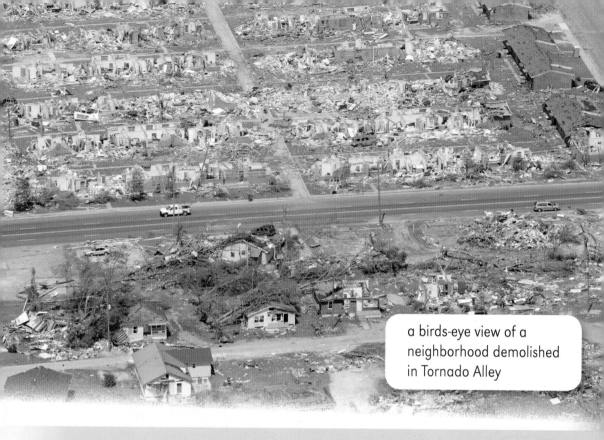

a birds-eye view of a neighborhood demolished in Tornado Alley

TED FUJITA AND THE F SCALE

In 1971 Dr Tetsuya Theodore "Ted" Fujita created the Fujita Scale. It was the first scale to measure the strength of a tornado. Fujita studied damage from tornadoes by flying over tornado-damaged areas. He inspected damage done to homes, cars, trees and fields. Fujita used general terms to describe the damage, such as "well-constructed homes levelled". Later in 2007 the Enhanced Fujita Scale replaced the Fujita Scale. The new scale describes in detail the degree of damage done to structures. For example, if experts are studying damage to a school, they would consider whether the windows and other fixtures were broken.

Forecasting tornadoes

Because tornadoes form so quickly and unpredictably, **forecasting** them as much as possible is very important. In the US, local and national weather services monitor approaching thunderstorms closely. They notify the public if conditions are present for tornadoes to form. A tornado watch means that tornadoes are likely to develop in a certain area. A tornado warning means that a tornado has been sighted. In places where tornadoes happen frequently, public tornado sirens often sound to warn people that they need to find shelter immediately.

Forecasters use tools such as the Doppler radar. The Doppler radar sends out radio waves that reflect off rain and hail and bounce back like an echo. Computers use this information to measure the storm's distance away and its intensity. **Satellites** can also take high-level photographs of clouds and storms. These images help forecasters locate areas with moist air where storms and supercells are likely to form.

SEEK SHELTER

What are the warning signs that a tornado could occur or is approaching?
- dark, often greenish sky
- large hail
- a large, dark, low-lying cloud where rotation is likely
- loud roar, similar to a freight train

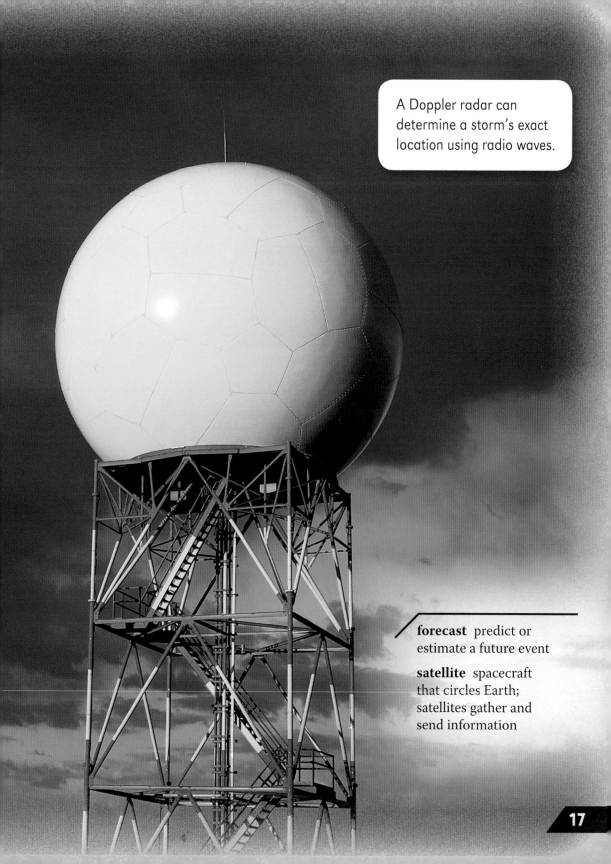

A Doppler radar can determine a storm's exact location using radio waves.

forecast predict or estimate a future event

satellite spacecraft that circles Earth; satellites gather and send information

THE WORLD'S WORST TORNADOES

In the United States

Because it sees so many tornadoes every year, the United States has also experienced some of the worst tornadoes in history. The worst US tornado travelled through Missouri, Illinois, and Indiana in 1925. Nicknamed the "Tri-State Tornado", the deadly twister was rated an EF5. Almost 700 people died, and more than 2,000 were injured.

On 20 May 2013, an EF5 tornado touched down in the town of Moore, Oklahoma. The tornado was 2.1 kilometres (1.3 miles) wide and stayed on the ground for 39 minutes. It travelled more than 23 kilometres (14 miles). The tornado killed 24 people, including seven children in a primary school. More than 200 people were injured. The twister crumbled roads and bridges and swept houses off their foundations. It was one of the costliest tornadoes in US history.

FACT

The killer Tri-State Tornado in 1925 travelled 352 kilometres (219 miles).

COSTLIEST US TORNADOES

Date	Place	Actual Cost
20 May 2013	Moore, Oklahoma	£1.5 billion
22 May 2011	Joplin, Missouri	£2.2 billion
27 April 2011	Tuscaloosa, Alabama	£1.9 billion
11 May 1970	Lubbock, Texas	£192 million
8 June 1966	Topeka, Kansas	£192 million

The Tri-State Tornado was the deadliest tornado in US history.

Around the globe

The United States may see the most tornadoes in the world, but powerful, deadly tornadoes often happen in other countries as well. The loss of life may be greater in places without good early-warning systems to help people get to safety before a tornado hits.

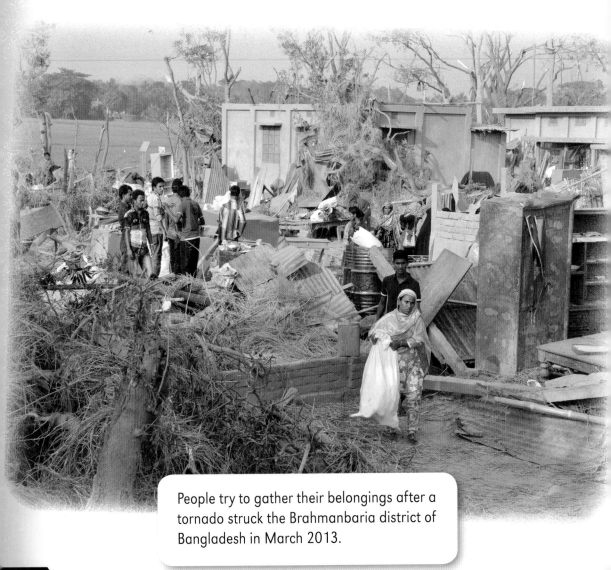

People try to gather their belongings after a tornado struck the Brahmanbaria district of Bangladesh in March 2013.

MAJOR TORNADO OUTBREAK

When several tornadoes form over a region, it is called an outbreak. The largest continuous and fourth-deadliest tornado outbreak in the United States was in 2011. A total of 362 tornadoes swept across 21 states from Texas to New York between 25 and 28 April. The most active day with a record 218 tornadoes was 27 April. The outbreak killed 324 people and injured more than 2,200.

In 1984 a severe tornado outbreak took place near Moscow in Russia. More than 10 tornadoes touched down in one day. These storms dropped pellets of hail that weighed an average of 0.9 kilograms (2 pounds) each. More than 400 people died. A couple of tornadoes in the outbreak were powerful enough to **disintegrate** concrete that was reinforced with steel.

In 1989 Bangladesh experienced its worst tornado in history. The tornado was 1.6 kilometres (1 mile) wide and injured more than 12,000 people. Around 80,000 people were left homeless. More deadly tornadoes hit Bangladesh in 1964, 1969, 1973 and 1977. These twisters killed a total of 2,341 people. The death tolls were high because many homes and shelters were fragile, and there wasn't an early-warning system.

disintegrate break into small pieces

STORM CHASERS AND SPOTTERS

Experts are always trying to find new ways to predict tornadoes and keep people safe. Some people specialize in watching storms and collecting information from them. In the United States, storm spotters are trained by the National Weather Service (NWS) to gather information about severe storms that take place near their homes. Then they report this information to the NWS. They report funnel clouds, tornadoes, the direction the storm is moving and the estimated wind speed.

Storm chasers travel to severe storms. Some chasers are scientists gathering weather data. Some are photographers or news reporters gathering photos and information for a story. The chasers risk being hurt by debris or even killed when a tornado unexpectedly forms and they are in its path. Some storm chasers have special armoured vehicles. The vehicles help them collect information but allow them to stay safe from being flipped over by the wind or hit by debris.

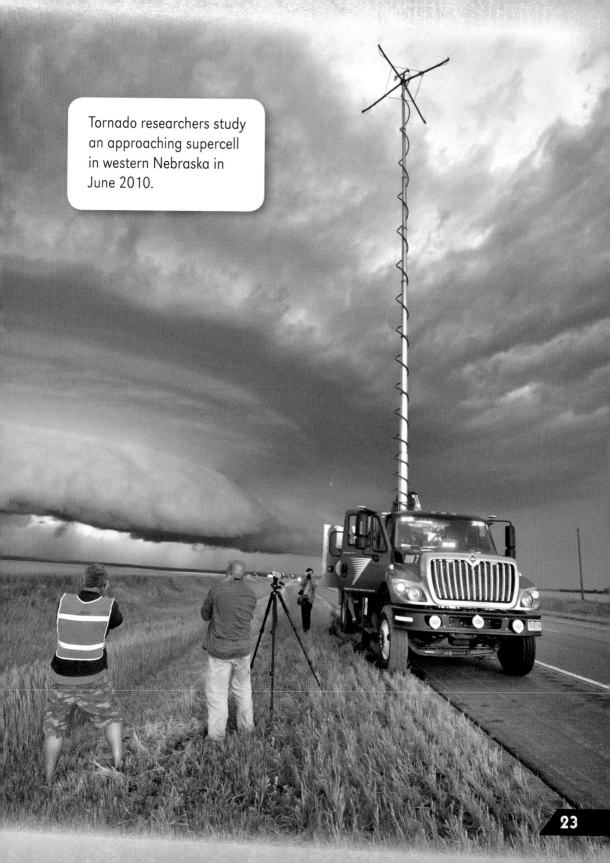

Tornado researchers study an approaching supercell in western Nebraska in June 2010.

Climate change

How will climate change affect tornadoes? Tornadoes are generated from thunderstorms, which feed on warm, moist air. These storms are created by low-level, unstable air. A warmer climate and warmer ocean water will create more of this unstable air. Increasing levels of **greenhouse gases** in the atmosphere also traps more heat on Earth's surface. This heat and moisture generate stronger storms and heavier rainfall.

Researchers have found that the number of days when large outbreaks of tornadoes occur has been increasing since 1950. And a larger number of tornadoes are occurring on those active days. With the world climate changing and shifting, tornado outbreaks could become more frequent.

greenhouse gases gases in a planet's atmosphere that trap heat energy from the sun

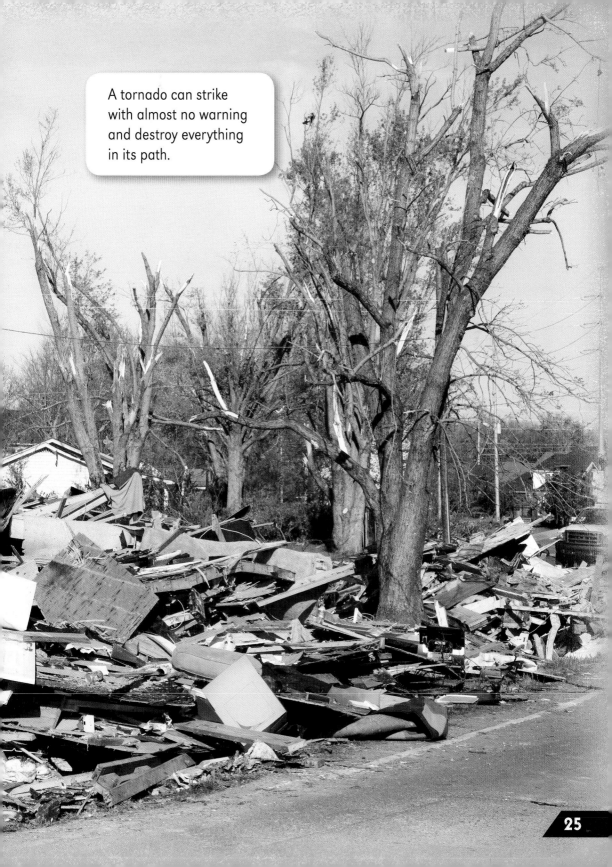

A tornado can strike with almost no warning and destroy everything in its path.

STAYING SAFE

Tornadoes can come out of nowhere. With some basic precautions and safety tips, you can keep yourself and your family safe. First, it is important to know where to go for safety if a tornado is heading your way. If a tornado siren goes off or a weather alert appears on the TV or radio, get to safety as quickly as possible.

If you are at home, you should go into the basement and get underneath something sturdy, such as a desk or table. If there is no basement, find a small interior room such as a bathroom. Stay away from windows. Crouch down, and cover your head with your hands.

If you live in a mobile home, do not stay there. Go to a sturdy building near by. If you are caught outside, find a ditch or a low place and lie down on your stomach. Cover your head with your hands.

FACT

Injuries from flying debris cause the most tornado-related deaths.

It is important to protect your head and face from falling or flying debris during a tornado.

Safety in the aftermath

A tornado often leaves behind piles of broken wood and jagged pieces of metal. There can be sharp objects in the rubble and debris left behind. Be careful when moving through tornado **wreckage**. Wear closed-toe shoes, long trousers and a long-sleeved top to protect yourself from cuts. Don't walk near to severely damaged buildings. These buildings are unsafe and could collapse.

After a tornado there is also the risk of electric shocks and fires. Stay away from fallen power lines. If you smell gas or hear a hissing sound in a home or building, get out quickly. Call the fire department or gas company to let them know a gas line might have broken.

Nothing can stop a tornado from coming. However, being prepared for its arrival and knowing how to stay safe afterwards can help to protect you and your family.

wreckage remains of something that has been badly damaged or destroyed

Do not approach fallen power lines because you could be electrocuted.

GLOSSARY

condense change from gas to liquid; water vapour condenses into liquid water

cumulonimbus cloud cloud that produces a thunderstorm

debris scattered pieces of something that has been destroyed or broken

destruction what happens when something is badly destroyed

disintegrate break into small pieces

evaporate change from a liquid to a gas

forecaster someone who calculates or predicts weather conditions

funnel cloud cone-shaped cloud that is usually a visible part of a tornado; a funnel cloud is wide at the top and narrow at the bottom

greenhouse gases gases in a planet's atmosphere that trap heat energy from the sun

satellite spacecraft that circles Earth; satellites gather and send information

wreckage remains of something that has been badly damaged or destroyed

READ MORE

I Survived the Joplin Tornado, 2011 (I Survived), Lauren Tarshis (Scholastic, 2015)

Science Vs Natural Disasters (Science Fights Back), Angela Royston (Raintree, 2016)

Storm Chasing (Xtreme Adventure), S. L. Hamilton (Franklin Watts, 2015)

WEBSITES

www.bbc.co.uk/science/earth/natural_disasters/tornado
Find out more about tornadoes by watching the video clips on the BBC Earth website.

news.bbc.co.uk/cbbcnews/hi/newsid_2290000/ newsid_2296600/2296605.stm
Watch this interactive guide to learn more about tornadoes.

www.ngkids.co.uk/science-and-nature/tornado-facts
Discover amazing facts and figures about tornadoes on the National Geographic children's website.

COMPREHENSION QUESTIONS

1. What specific conditions are needed for a tornado to form?

2. How are tornadoes measured? Describe the system.

3. How could climate change affect the weather?

INDEX